finest digital art in the known universe

Created and Edited by

Mark Snoswell & Leonard Teo

EXPOSÉ 1

Published
by
Ballistic Publishing

Publishers of digital works for the digital world.

Aldgate Valley Rd
Mylor SA 5153
Australia

www.BallisticPublishing.com

Correspondence:
info@BallisticPublishing.com

First Edition published in Australia 2003 by Ballistic Publishing

National Library of Australia Cataloguing-in-Publication entry
    Exposé 1 : finest art in the known universe.
    Includes index.
    ISBN 0 9750965 0 8 (limited ed.).
    ISBN 0 9750965 1 6.
    ISBN 0 9750965 2 4 (pbk.).
    1. Computer art. 2. Computer graphics. I. Snoswell, Mark Andrew. II. Teo, Leonard.
    741.60285

Editors: Mark Snoswell & Leonard Teo
Producer: Helen Snoswell
Art Director and Layout: Mark Snoswell
Image Processing: Sam Hodge and Damien Snelgrove

Advisory board: Steven Stahlberg, Pascal Blanché, Alex Alvarez, Robert "Lunatique" Chang, Kirt Stanke, William "Proton" Vaughan, Tito "Lildragon" Belgrave, Jeff Mottle.

Printed in Adelaide, Australia by Hyde Park Press: www.hydeparkpress.com.au
Limited Collectors Edition bound by Chasdor Bindery, Adelaide, Australia

Affiliates:
CGNetworks - www.CGNetworks.com, www.CGTalk.com
cgCharacter - www.cgCharacter.com

/ **BALLISTIC** /

Mark Snoswell

Mark Snoswell

Leonard Teo

Leonard Teo

As we write this editorial, EXPOSÉ has already become a phenomenal global success. It has been sold in over 43 countries worldwide and received critical acclaim from all quarters around the world -- all before a single copy has shipped! In every way EXPOSÉ is a pivotal event in the history of publication of art and many of you reading this are a part of that history in the making. From concept to content to design to publication and even distribution EXPOSÉ is a product of the digital age.

We were told that you should "learn to walk before you run". Not only did we skip the walking phase, we went ballistic from day one! The traditional concept of "getting up and running" is archaic in the face of digital technology. You can forget walking, running or any mode of ground transport as a metaphor. Running is for apes, we've gone ballistic and we're going into orbit! EXPOSÉ is a publication of new millennium art created by a new generation of technically savvy artists.

As you view these pages you see an eclectic collection of work from around the world. The images range from architectural visualizations created by the world's leading design firms to a wealth of images from established professionals and many, many unknown and very young artists. In an attempt to salvage some order from a rampant explosion of digital talent, we have loosely imposed categories that group work into 2D and 3D in genres that reflect current digital art industries.

Reflecting the blank canvas of a dead screen, EXPOSÉ starts with a black page. Like the artists who poured their creative talents in to images that fill these pages, we have drawn upon every digital tool and clever piece of software to create something that is new and is the best. We've also leveraged the digital world to collect, design, create, publish, market and distribute EXPOSÉ at the speed of light. We're going to frighten a lot of traditional publishers because we appear to have come out of the blue and done something great in a blink of their eye. Many of the artists celebrated on these pages have done no less. More than anything else it's a blast to feature so many unknown artists from around the world in a premium global publication. For all of us together -- the future looks very bright indeed.

Going digital is not about the tools, the style or abandoning everything you've known before. It's about freedom. Freedom from the confining rules of physical media. Freedom to try anything, to do things a new way. Freedom to work at the speed of light. But perhaps, most of all, it's about the freedom that allows anyone from anywhere in the world to learn and develop their talents and to participate in a global community of like minded people. Nowhere is this more obvious than in 3D. Here artists can imagine and create their own 3D worlds and creatures. It's our greatest regret that all we can do is show you still snapshots of 3D work. However we have tried to select those images that are not just technically merited but more importantly reveal artistic talent. The digital storm of 3D creation has not blown out the artistic spirit, rather is has fanned the fires of creation and revealed the soul of both artists and their creations alike.

It's almost July 2003 now. It was less than 3 months ago in April we decided to form our own publishing business. As a start, we wanted to draw on, and to promote, the artistic talents of the 250,000+ unique artists that visit our forums on www.CGTalk.com every month. It took just one week to establish Ballistic Publishing and to get a call for entries going. Entries poured in. In the first two weeks we selected 18 entries and printed 8,000 Call For Entry cards that were distributed at the 3D Festival in Copenhagen in May. We started on the book design just 23 days ago on June 1st. The advisory board helped us sort through 1,400 entries and select winners in 10 categories plus a Grand Master. Today the book went to press and it will ship to everywhere around the world in just 4 weeks. We have a string of new books lined up to release before EXPOSÉ 2 next year, which already looks like it will be huge! We called ourselves Ballistic Publishing for a reason. Please enjoy our first publication and look out for us in orbit very soon with more!

ARCHITECTURE

The Cedar Trace Residence. 3ds max
John Pruden, USA

Computer Aided Design (CAD) is one of the earliest 3D graphical applications. However at the outset it was designed to output blueprints and to estimate materials, neither involved creating images of any appeal. That has all changed at an astounding pace over the past few years. Architectural Visualization is now the single fastest growing segment of the 3D industry. Almost 25% of all entries submitted for judging in the EXPOSÉ Awards were architectural renders. Beyond the normal assistance of the advisory board the help of Jeff Mottle from CGarchitect (www.cgarchitect.com) was invaluable.

The architectural renders we received were of a consistently high technical quality. While many entrants struggled with rendering at print resolution, the architects clearly had no trouble. In fact, some of the architectural renders were positively massive with resolutions exceeding 10,000 pixels horizontally and vertically!

It was a pleasant suprise to see individual professionals and even students holding their own amongst the strong showing of images from many of the world's leading architectural and design companies.

This section more than most exhibits a great deal of raw technical excellence. However, you can see that a a lot of effort also goes into making these visualizations appealing. Great care goes into dressing the 3D sets with people, foliage and general landscaping. This area also demands attention to camera optics and advanced lighting techniques to deliver both an appealing image and an accurate reflection of the real world – photographically and photometrically accurate in some cases!

CHARACTER in REPOSE

KiloByte. 3ds max
Marcin Skrzypczak, Poland

Our goal with the Character in Repose category was to showcase organic or mechanical characters that demonstrate the ability of the artist to bring that character to life. This encompassed technical skill, believability, composition and emotion.

In terms of entry numbers, this category was dominated by digital illustrations of an overall high quality. The mixture of styles was truly refreshing, showing the artists' ability to use the digital medium as a means of creative expression. The advent of the "natural media" paint software Painter and highly responsive digitising tablets and pens from Wacom have had a massive impact

in this area. WIth Painter the artist can not only accurately emulate any natural media, they can go beyond what they could ever dream of doing within the confines of the physical world.

The quality of 3D entries in this category varied tremendously from very poor to fantastic, with few at the fantastic end of the scale. We believe the main reason for this is the complexity of 3D software compared to 2D illustration software. 3D software and the range of skills required is phenomenally complex and difficult to master. It's not until after you master modelling, mapping, texturing, lighting, camera and several other

skills that your innate artistic talent can emerge unscathed from a technical failing in any one of these areas. 3D is easy to get into but extremely difficult to master! In too many cases, we also received obvious technical tests of characters in neutral poses showing no artistic merit or attempt at creative expression.

Technical issues aside, this category showcases some of the most beautiful and inspiring works of digital character art ever.

CHARACTER in ACTION

They're bananas, Reverend. 3ds max
Jimmy Maidens, USA

Submissions of characters leaned very much towards the still pose. It was relatively rare to see artists capturing a character in action. In this category we were looking for the rare talent that succeeded in capturing an expressive motion frozen in a moment in time, evoking the sheer power, energy or elegance of a character in motion. Regrettably many artists, particularly in the 3D area, fell back to putting their characters in a relatively artifical pose, even when the character was meant to be in the middle of some action. When we did get a real action snapshot it was quite amazing to see just how much more power and emotion it conveyed. It was also disappointing that we did not get more than a very few 3D shots

with motion or camera blur or other special effects to convey action. Motion and camera blur are common techniques in the rendering of 3D animations, but it is a rare artist who is brave enough to blur their precious single still render and thus we lost a lot of potential power and emotion from many of the entries we saw.

There is probably another reason for the relative dearth of character in action images. That's because it's simply much more technically difficult to depict motion. This is extremely so for 3D characters. As we noted for Characters in Repose, there are a large number of areas of technical expertise that have to be mastered to even create

a still 3D character that is believable and engaging. It's not just twice as hard to make those characters move well -- it's many, many times harder. Although we are deluged by 3D imagery these days the whole industry is still relatively new and certainly technically difficult to master.

Notably, this category attracted a number of entries from games and visual effects studios such as Spellcraft Studios, Framestore CFC and Oddworld Inhabitants. With today's software it often takes a large team of people to truly bring an animated character to life. Games and films can afford to create virtual 3D stars with big teams of artists.

ENVIRONMENT

Coast. Photoshop
Seung Ho Henrik Holmberg, Sweden

The goal for this category is to showcase the best artistic display of sets or locations. This could be indoors, outdoors, underwater, in space – anywhere. At its essence is the artist's ability to evoke a sense of wonder, making viewers want to see more of this world.

There are four loose groups of images that make up this category. The first overlaps with architectural renderings but with more of a focus on a complete outdoor setting than you find in the normal architectural images. The second is matte paintings used as backdrops for film work. The third is 3D renders of sets for games or film. The final group is images that fit

none of the first three work-related groups, but rather are simply wonderful evocative images of some setting or place.

The 2D environment is the only category in which there are two Master Awards. In addition to the Master Award won by Justin Cherry we have also honoured Seung Ho Henrik Holmberg for his extraordinary display of matte paintings. The jury was torn between the evocative beauty of Justin's winning image "The Lost Watchtower" and the consistent and prolific grandeur of Seung Ho's work. Both artists submitted images of Master standard and we have chosen to honour them both as Masters in this area.

This is probably a good time to also point out that some of the matte painting works that we do feature in the book are truly massive in both their size and their technical detail. Even with a full spread image you still can't appreciate the vast detail in these images. The other extraordinary thing is how photo-real these matte images look, even though they are painted. This is of course the very intent of a matte painting -- that it serves as a background image for a film, in place of footage of a "real" scene.

Overall, this was a stunning category, chock-full of fantastic, awe-inspiring worlds.

MECHANICAL

Minidisc player. 3ds Max, Rhino
**Jonatan Catalán Navarrete &
Victor Ruiz Santacruz,** Spain.

In the very new industry of 3D, computer aided mechanical design (CAD) and product visualisation are perhaps the most venerable variants. Unfortunately we only reached a few people in this market segment with our call for entries. With so few entries in this area we combined still life with this category. This brought in a number of the highly technical "3D render test" images. It was gratifying to see that amongst the great wealth of mundane technical render tests we are starting to see some very elegant still life images. These images are even more impressive if you are familiar with the process involved to create them -- they are truly on the cutting edge of 3D rendering technology.

The past few years has seen an explosion of 3D rendering techniques and renderers. A common thread amongst these new renderers is improvements in their ability to accommodate physically accurate lights and photometrically correct environmental lighting. The specific techniques here are Global Illumination (GI) and support for High Dynamic Range Images (HDRI). We believe that HDRI image support is going to have the single greatest impact on the way 3D rendering is done in the next few years -- perhaps in the next decade. The vast majority of computer graphics is currently 24 bit, that is 8 bits (256 levels) for red, green and blue. HDRI images use a floating point representation of each of the

red, green and blue. This means that there is no practical limit to the exposure range they can encode in a single image. It is now possible to capture an HDRI image of a real world location that has all the light and colour information about that scene -- even if that includes a bright sun through to deep shadow information. That HDRI image can now be used as the complete environment for a 3D rendering. As the HDRI image accurately encodes all of the lighting in a scene there is no need for "computer" lights.

STILL LIFE

d'aroma chair. 3ds max, finalRender
Mario Rothenbühler, Switzerland

This category was included with Mechanical as we had such a small number of suitable entries in these categories. There were several reasons for this: our call for entries didn't reach as many product designers as we would have liked; there are simply not as many still life and mechanical renders done in general; many of the entries for still life were not suitable. This last point is worthy of comment. We did receive quite a number of human head studies. These are 3D renderings of heads in a neutral pose. Many artists aspire to create a realistic human (or at least humanoid) head as their starting point. This is a very exciting thing to do now as we are on the very edge of being able to create totally

realistic humans relatively easily. We have seen the first digital human performances in limited short appearances at technical conferences and some public shows. Soon we will see totally realistic computer generated humans in major appearances -- first in film. This is all very exciting, however, in the vast majority of cases the quality (lack of) and artistic merit of these technical head renders do not make them suitable for a publication like this.

Another area that is driving the re-emergence of the 3D still life is the emerging capabilities to do ever more realistic renders of real life -- including HDRI imaging, refraction, atmospheric light

scattering and radiosity. People are also realizing that 3D renders should be viewed just like a raw photograph and are doing heavy post-processing of their images. Traditionally this is done in Adobe Photoshop. However the advent of HDRI imaging and rendering has vastly surpassed the capabilities of Photoshop. Photoshop works very well and enjoys a virtual monopoly on the image processing industry, but it has no abilities to cope with HDRI images and renders. For the first time we are seeing a surge in the capability of alternate image processing software with many people choosing to use film compositing software like Combustion and Digital Fusion for image processing of HDRI images and renders.

TRANSPORT

Uniracers. 3ds max
Richard Green, USA

There are many ways of getting from one place to another, if you use your imagination! Although there was an over-abundance of photo-realistic cars entered, the judges were amazed with the more creative modes of transportation, including the "Uniracers" image by Richard Green (above), which took the Master award.

The majority of work submitted for the Transport category was 3D, with many from games and television commercials, perhaps reflecting the high demand for photo-realistic cars in these markets. There were a few space ships and war machines to add to the mix, but the most interesting were the 'alternative' means of transportation such as

the "OneHorse OpenSleigh" by Howard Gersh and "Kamikazi Cockroach" by Todd Dewsnup (both on page 174).

Although all areas of 3D are advancing at breakneck pace, we have seen games push the boundaries of realism furthest. Game developers wil always strive to use every ounce of that available computing power. If you are working on a character-based game then there is quite a lot of resources devoted to deforming the soft bodies of characters, rendering their hair and clothing. To make characters even more realistic will also require rendering correct translucent skin. All of these things are difficult and consume vast

amounts of programming resources and computer power. In comparison, the rigid surfaces of cars and their glossy duco paint finishes are much easier and less demanding to do. As a consequence it is possible to really push the degree of realism of the cars and other rigid body vehicles in games.

The same holds true for rendering cars for broadcast commercials and for film. Unless you are part of the 3D and effects industry, you are probably not even aware that in movies like 'Driven', many of the racing cars are not "real". Photoreal computer generated cars are used heavily to create shots that would be physically impossible, prohibitively expensive or too dangerous.

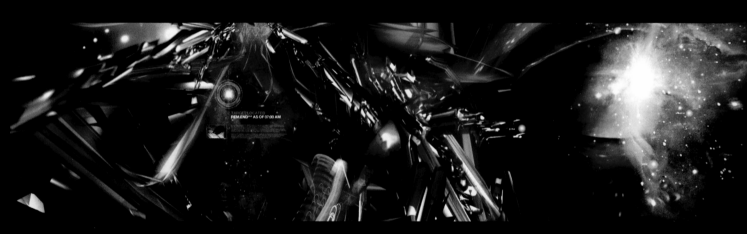

VISUAL EFFECT

Dreamweaver. 3ds max, Photoshop
Jens Karlsson, Sweden

OK. We made a mistake when we thought we would get a lot of entries for this category. We got very few, and certainly not the types of images we were expecting. When we drew up the requirements for this category we were thinking of the 3D effects industry. Here you have visual effects like fire, smoke, water, particles, image distortion and a host of others. You don't tend to notice these as they are often not the center of attention but there are very many great effects in recent films that come to mind.

If you have seen any of the great effects movies then you have watched and enjoyed seeing a vast parade of visual effects in the form of explosions,

waterfalls and raging rivers, dust, foliage, light scattering, tornadoes ... the list goes on and on.

FIlms, broadcast and other high profile games work all generate a host of special effects. What we didn't take into account, though, was that these high profile projects also have legal and marketing departments that make it very hard to get clearance to use images in most cases. So while we know the artists who have done the actual work on many of the recent high profile projects, that doesn't mean a thing when it comes to getting clearance for them to submit their images. This was compounded by the extremely short time we had to get this book out

to meet our deadline of late July -- in time for the SIGGRAPH conference in San Diego.

The result of all these factors is that this categor is small and contains an extremely diverse rang of 3D and 2D images that can only very loosely b grouped as visual effects.

Sunday Fluff XX. 3ds max. **Jimmy Maidens**, USA

The entries varied tremendously, from something like the one above to the one below -- from one person's fantasy to someones else's you could say. However there are a preponderance of female subjects in the images -- human or not.

We do have some truly phenomenal female artists' work featured -- like the award winning work from Linda Bergkvist who won the Master Award in the Character in Repose 2D category. But although there is a good showing of non-testosterone laden work

in the 2D categories, sadly the 3D categories are dominated by boys -- boys who never seem to grow up or tire of creating their own dream women ;) So come on girls: let's see more of you and your work gracing the pages of future editions of EXPOSÉ .

Insatiable Appetites. Photoshop. **Malachi D. Maloney**, USA

Leonard Teo | Founder and Administrator
CGTalk.com

Tito A. Belgrave | Director of Community
Development. CGTalk.com

CGTalk is the international web forum for CGI (computer generated imagery) professionals and aspirants alike. Established in December 2002, CGTalk has rapidly grown into one of the largest online communities dedicated to CGI and digital art. It's become a popular site for digital artists to showcase their work and obtain constructive critique from peers. CGTalk is also home to one of the largest online galleries for peer reviewed, high quality artwork.

As CGTalk grew, we found a disturbing trend in that much of the excellent work posted was lost over time. This could be due to technical reasons or the simple fact that the Web is a dynamic and volatile medium. Nothing is static on the Web and, from what we have experienced, web content comes and goes.

Using CGTalk as the focal point, we wanted to collect and promote the best of the huge volume of truly excellent artwork that is being generated all the time over a whole range of related industries. The idea for a book, EXPOSÉ (pronounced 'ex-pose-ay'), came from two people -- Leonard Teo and his friend and mentor Mark Snoswell. The idea was to create a definitive volume of the best digital artwork collected with the help of the CGTalk community.

CGTalk played a pivotal role in the foundation of EXPOSÉ. The advisory committee consisted of forum moderators and prolific community members, who oversaw the establishment of the EXPOSÉ Awards. CGTalk also served as the main collection point for all of the artwork for EXPOSÉ. Using an online registration system on CGTalk, artists were able to upload their artwork for EXPOSÉ consideration.

CGTalk and EXPOSÉ share a symbiotic relationship. As CGTalk grew in leaps and bounds, we felt the pinch when needing to improve our server capabilities to handle the flood of new members. Having extensive experience in the Web industry, we understood that banner advertising was not going to keep CGTalk running, given the amount of resources needed to maintain it. Ballistic Publishing is going to take on funding the continual running and improvement of CGTalk, using the proceeds from EXPOSÉ and future book sales. This will ensure that CGTalk will continue to improve and provide an open forum for digital artists from all walks of life to come together free from the absolute reliance on advertisers and sponsors.

EXPOSÉ is a milestone for the CG industry and we're thrilled that CGTalk has played such a pivotal role in its founding. As we look to the future, we see the continual proliferation of digital art, and we look forward to playing our part in representing the voice of the international CG community at large.

The Fury. ZBrush, Photoshop, **Steve Townsend**, UK

Craig Mullins

When we went to select a Grand Master for this premiere edition of EXPOSÉ, we knew we would be making history and needed to find someone astoundingly talented, someone focused on the digital medium, with broad appeal & range of talents, someone approachable who had made a major contribution to digital art, and the whole of art in general. The work of one outstanding individual met and even exceeded all of our criteria.

When we asked for nominations the entire advisory board already knew of Craig's work and instantly nominated him -- we raced off to visit his web site and came back astounded!

While we could fill a book with the wealth of diverse and moving images from this one artist, Craig has selected a few for us to display here. Readers are encouraged to visit Craig's web site at www.goodbrush.com and feast upon the staggering array of work from this one artist.

So it is with great pleasure that we celebrate the talent that is Craig Mullins and the contribution that he has made to the digital art world by honouring him with the inaugural EXPOSÉ Grand Master Award.

-- The Editors.

Craig was born in sunny California in the mid sixties only to be moved to Ohio at the tender age of 3. It took him another 15 years to return to California where, at the age of 18, he attended Pitzer College in Claremont for two years, followed by the Art Center College of Design to study product design. Never one to conform, Craig was better at drawing cars than products. This led to an internship at Ford. Alas, Craig's design sense was a little weird to be of any value to anybody in Detroit, so he returned, once again, to the Art Center to study illustration. Craig had a bout

Craig (top right) at home in Hawaii with his daughter Molly (bottom) and his cat Kat (left).

of conservatism and refined his academic skills of drawing and painting, eventually graduating in 1990.

Craig was first introduced to the computer at Ford in '87 in the form of a "Dubner PaintBox.", which did pretty much what Photoshop does. Later, while working for a short time at a big effects house, Craig was introduced to Photoshop by one of its creators, John Knoll. From '94 on Craig has done all his commercial work digitally. He started doing a lot of digital concept painting for architects and theme parks and that slowly led to contacts within the film business. Craig was then doing mostly matte paintings until about '98 when he felt that the growth of 3D made it clear that matte work was going to be largely replaced in the near future. Until then, he had coasted on what he had learned in school. Craig made the choice to go back to the fundamentals of drawing and painting from life in an attempt to diversify what he could offer to clients. Now Craig is the master of many different styles and types of work -- thinking that if any one lessens the others will pick up the slack.

A few years ago Craig realized that his clients were global and the digital era had freed him to work from anywhere in the world -- and so he fulfilled a long time dream and now lives in Hawaii with his wife Jennifer, daughter Molly and cat Kat.

Craig's Artwork

Lost in Green (this page) - "I think I did a number of these 'lost in the green' images after moving to the tropics. Self-portraits of me lost in the jungle? I try to invoke a sort of intoxication with my images, with a sensory overload that blots out rational thought. I suppose that is the definition of Romanticism. I try to balance the naturalistic with the fantastic, and they can play off each other if you are doing well."

Pirates (next page) - "The pirate images that I do could be one part vicarious living, one part figure study, one part tongue in cheek. I try not to take illustration too seriously, and these are just me having fun. Also pirates tended to be malnourished, so you can see the bone structure pretty clearly. I love the

Brandywine tradition of storytelling, and I believe these fit into that genre. But to keep the viewer interested, I think there has to be some ambiguity involved. When I can load up the image with things that can support a variety of storylines it brings the viewer more into the image. It is also a lot more challenging than spelling out everything."

Woodward Hotel
Client: Woodward Hotel
Photoshop
Andy Hickes, Rendering.net, USA

LakeTown Golfcourse
LightWave, Photoshop
Tajino, Clickgrafix, Malaysia

1
Crystal City Retail South
Client: Charles E Smith Realty Companies
AccuRender, Photoshop
Vincent M Hunter,
WDG Habib Architecture, USA

2
Ice Discotheque
Client: PT. Susanto Ciptajaya, Jakarta,
Indonesia
AutoCAD, 3ds max
3DesignArchitect, Indonesia/Australia

3
Mixed Use Commercial Building - Indonesia
Client: PT Susanto Ciptajaya, Jakarta,
Indonesia
AutoCAD, 3ds max
3DesignArchitect, Indonesia/Australia

4
Look up at the Sky
AutoCAD, Lightscape
Chen Qingfeng, China

1

2

1

1
St Thamas Street
Client: Sellar Properties
3ds max, Photoshop
Hayes Davidson, UK

2
Telenor Fornebu Atrium
Client: Telenor
MicroStation, Lightscape, Photoshop
Dag Jomar Meyer, Kim Baumann Larsen, Lars Ribbum,
Nazare Lillebø & Jonathan Ward,
PLACEBO EFFECTS & NBBJ-HUS-PKA Architects, Norway

3
Clubhouse at Hawk's Prairie
Client: Biltform Architectural Group
3ds max, VRay, Photoshop
John Pruden, Digital-X, USA

4
Vertical Village - Bioclimatic tower
3ds max, Photoshop
Igor Knezevic, Flare Group, USA

2

3

1

1
Carlyon Bay - typical apartment interior
Client: Ampersand
3ds max, Lightscape, Photoshop
Jon Hey, Smoothe, UK

2
Space
Lightscape
Chen Qingfeng, China

3
Dragon's Gate Bridge
Client: Parsons Brinckerhoff
3ds max, Photoshop
Glen Loyd & Scott Danielson,
Company 39, USA

4
400 George St - Sydney
Client: Alpha Multimedia
LightWave, Photoshop
David A. Wright & Anthony A. Wright,
Artmaze, USA

2

3

1
Country Club
3ds max, Photoshop
focus360, USA

2
Nara Spa Lobby
LightWave, Photoshop
Tajino, Clickgrafix, Malaysia

3
Residential Housing 'Het Volk'
Client: G+D Studiegroep Bontinck
3ds max, Photoshop
AniMotionS, Belgium

4
Richemont: Cartier Headquarters Geneva
Client: Richemont Group
AutoCAD, 3ds max, Photoshop
Andrew Hartness,
Ateliers Jean Nouvel, France

5
Pre-show Dining Area
Client: Guthrie Theater
AutoCAD, 3ds max, Photoshop
Andrew Hartness,
Ateliers Jean Nouvel, France

© 2003 focus360

2

1
New City Arts Campus Competition for LaSalle-SIA
Client: HASSELL (Singapore) with DCA
AutoCAD, 3ds max
3DesignArchitect, Indonesia/Australia

2
Residential Building at Tempe Town Lake
Client: Biltform Architectural Group
3ds max, VRay, Photoshop
John Pruden, Digital-X, USA

3
Alberti square
Client: ARX , Paolo Di Nardo Architect
form•Z, CINEMA 4D, Photoshop
Fabrizio Pascucci, Simbiosi, Italy

4
Mosque Precint 3
LightWave , Photoshop
Tajino, Clickgrafix, Malaysia

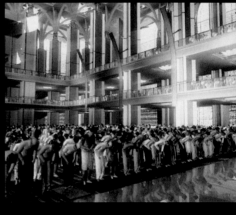

1
Nightdrama
3ds max, Photoshop
Adam Howard, Invisiblecities, UK

2
Art Centre Design Competition
AutoCAD, 3ds max,
3DesignArchitect,
Indonesia/Australia

3
A Space for Civic Rituals / 4D
AutoCAD, 3ds max, finalRender,
Photoshop
Dimitar Karanikolov, Bulgaria

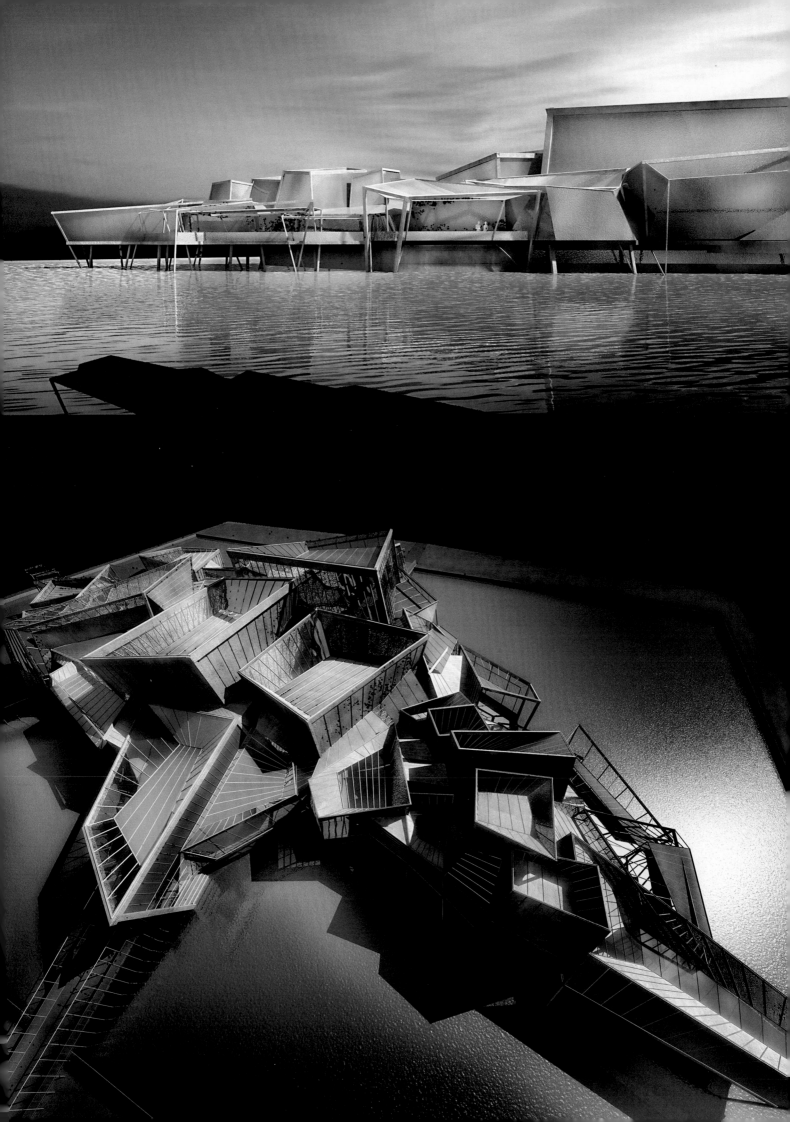

1

1
Sports Center in Kaunas, Lithuania
Client: Architectural bureau
Vilius ir Partneriai
ArchiCAD, Art·lantis
Dalius Regelskis,
UAB Design Solutions, Lithuania

2
*Reception area of the proposed
NCSU Alumni Center*
Client: NCSU Alumni Association
AutoCAD, 3ds max
**William J. Blackmon &
Gennadiy T'omin**,
Command Digital Studios, USA.

3
*WASPS (Workshop & Artists'
Studio Provision Scotland)
Headquarters*
Client: WASPS Arts Charity
VIZ, Photoshop
Steve Colmer, Soluis, UK

4
Interior Illumination
3ds max, finalRender, Photoshop
Xiaoyong Lee, Killcat, China

5.
Daylight
Lightscape
Chen Qingfeng, China

2

3

1
Temple
Client: Park + Associates,
Singapore
AutoCAD, 3ds max
3DesignArchitect,
Indonesia/Australia

2
Private Home
Client: Freitas & Assoc
3ds max, Photoshop
Sawyer Fischer,
Sawyer Fischer Rendering, USA

3
The Cedar Trace Residence
Client: AIM Properties
3ds max, VRay, Photoshop
John Pruden, Digital-X, USA

4 & 5
Shah Alam Round-about
LightWave, Photoshop
Tajino, Clickgrafix, Malaysia

1
Edificio Tenis
Client: Promociones Garcia Belillo
LightWave
Juan Jose Gonzalez Diaz, Spain

2
Townhouse Project
Client: Park + Associates, Singapore
AutoCAD, 3ds max
3DesignArchitect, Indonesia/Australia

3
Valet - Kuta Galleria
Client: PT. Kuta Galeri Gemilang
AutoCAD, 3ds max
3DesignArchitect, Indonesia/Australia

4
Broadway - Kuta Galleria
Client: PT. Kuta Galeri Gemilang,
Indonesia
AutoCAD, 3ds max
3DesignArchitect, Indonesia/Australia

1

2

3

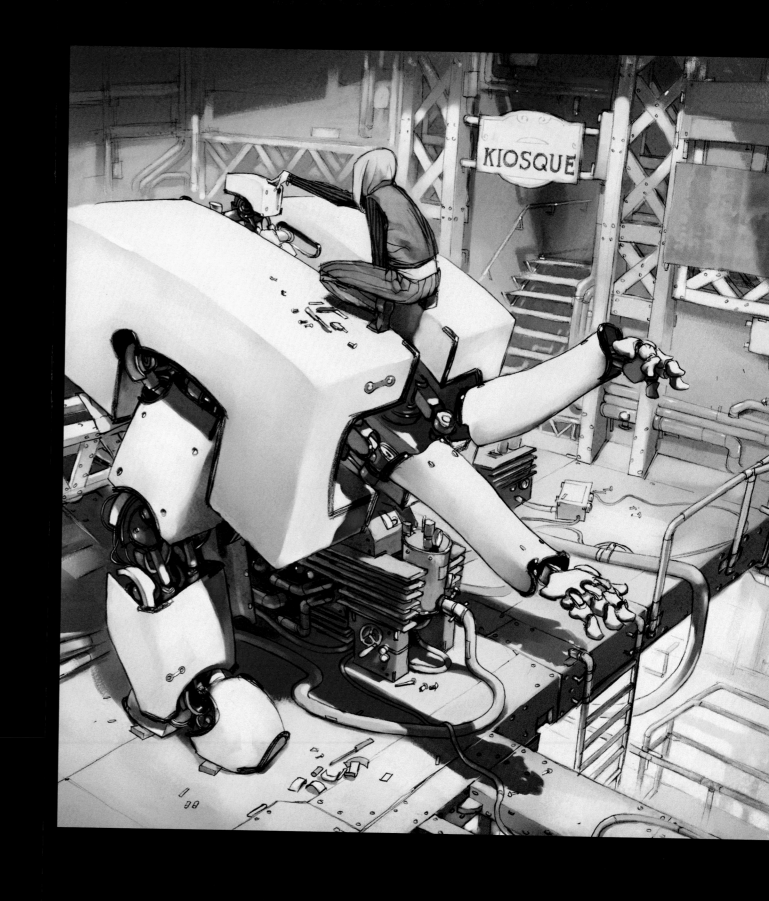

Fixing Joe

1
Love Devotion - A Painting with love for Valentine
Painter
Kong Foong Ching, The One Academy, Malaysia

2
Sorina Redfeather
Photoshop, Poser
Kevin Moore, USA

3
Angel
Photoshop
Pierre St-Hilaire, My Virtual Model, Canada

3

1
A Birth ("Yes. don't worry, papa")
Photoshop
Seung-hee Lee, South Korea

2
Nausicaa - inspired by Hayao Miyazaki anime
Photoshop
Jiaxing Rong, USA

3
Silverback
Photoshop
Stephen Otvos,
Otvos Illustration, Canada

1
Scythe Wolf
Painter, Photoshop
Robert Chang, USA

2
Spectre 6
Photoshop
James Hawkins,
Legend Entertainment, USA

3
the Creation
Photoshop
Joel F. Thomas, USA

4
Cemetary Dance
Photoshop
Kyri Koniotou, UK

5
Eclipse
Photoshop, Painter
Kym hyun-seung, Korea

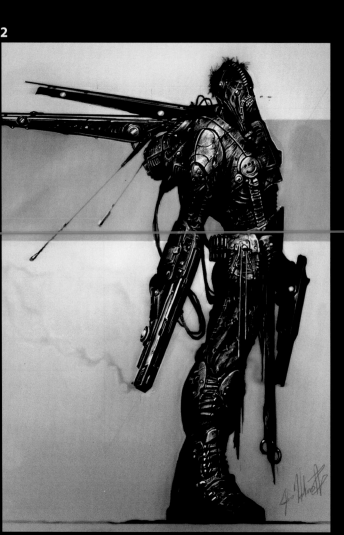

1
Self-Portrait, or On the Gender of Angels and Red Vegetables
Photoshop
Christos Neofotistos, Greece

2
Centurian
Photoshop
Stephen Otvos, Otvos Illustration, Canada

3
Nelicquele
Photoshop, Painter
Linda Bergkvist, Sweden

1

2

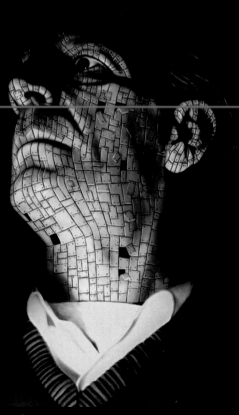

3

1

2

3

2

3

2

3

1
Shotgun Messiah
Photoshop
Chris Koutroulos, Greece

2
Electra
Photoshop
Chris Koutroulos, Greece

3
Lara My Love
Client: Eidos Interactive/Core Design
PhotoShop, LightWave
Danny Geurtsen, UK

4
Heavy Hitter
Photoshop
Don Perkins, Don Perkins Illustration, USA

Mermaid
3ds max, Photoshop
Pascal Blanché, Ubisoft, Canada

Lady Bird
CINEMA 4D, BodyPaint, Photoshop
Péter Fendrik, Hungary

1

1
Enchanted
Client: Keyframe Magazine
LightWave
Timothy Albee,
Timothy Albee Fine Art/Animation, USA

2
AlienBob
Maya
Matthew Dartford, UK

3
Hook
ZBrush
Marcel Laverdet, France

2

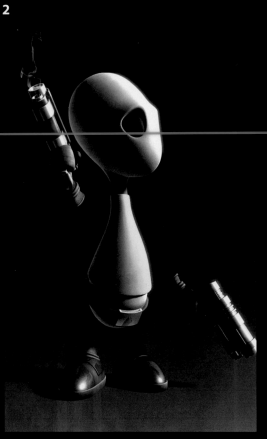

3

kingston   west indies   circa 1688

Kishars
3ds max, Photoshop

1
Living Toon
3ds max, VRay, Photoshop
Ila Soleimani, Iran

2
Oddworld Inhabitants - Bad Ending
Maya, Shake, Photoshop
**Oddworld CG & Production Design
Departments**, USA

3
T R U S T
Maya, Photoshop
Dany Bittel, Switzerland

2

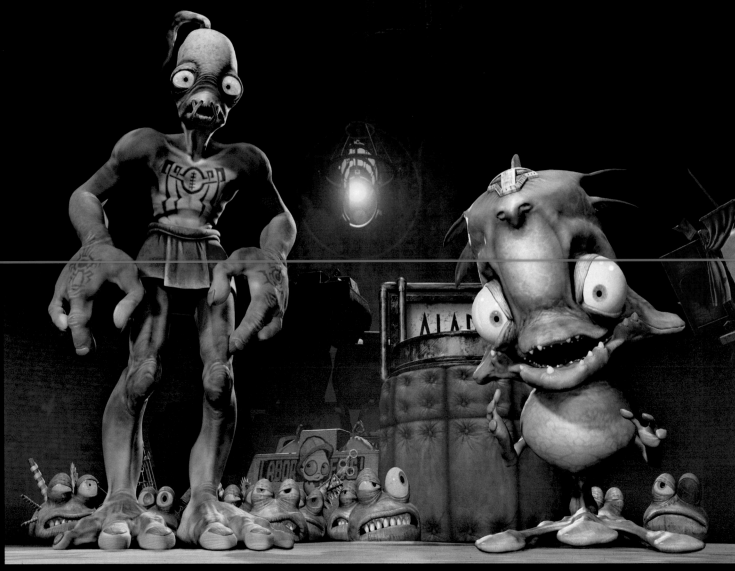

1
Mantis
LightWave, Photoshop
Grzegorz Jonkajtys, Poland

2
Acanthoscurria
3ds max, Brazil
Giubelli Marco, MysticMan Productions, Italy

3
Trichius
3ds max, Brazil
Giubelli Marco, MysticMan Productions, Italy

4
the LilB's
LightWave, Photoshop
Anders Ehrenborg, Sweden

5
Within the Tall Grass
Client: Wordware Publishing
LightWave
Timothy Albee, Timothy Albee Fine Art/Animation, USA

3

4

1
Crossroads
Maya, Arnold
Mario Tarradas & Edu Martín,
Pixel in Motion, Spain

2
The Secret Joys of Myopia
Maya, 3ds max, finalRender,
After Effects
Keith Lango,
Keith Lango Animation, USA

3
Poor Bogo
Maya, Shake, RenderMan,
Premiere, Photoshop
Thelvin Cabezas, Ringling School
of Art and Design, Costa Rica

4
Forestia
Maya, Deep Paint, Photoshop
Kang Dong-Hyun,
Wizard Soft, Korea

1
Savage Warrior
3ds max, Brazil, Photoshop
Juan Jose, Spain

2
Magdalenian
ZBrush
Marcel Laverdet, France

3
Sidekick
3ds max, Photoshop
Sami Salo, Finland

4
Male character
LightWave, Photoshop
Jacques Defontaine, Belgium

1
Cyan
Maya, Photoshop
Jane Wong, Malaysia

2
Code K-1
LightWave, Photoshop,
HDR Shop
Christelle Rouchaville,
France

3
End of the line
LightWave
Werner Ziemerink,
South Africa

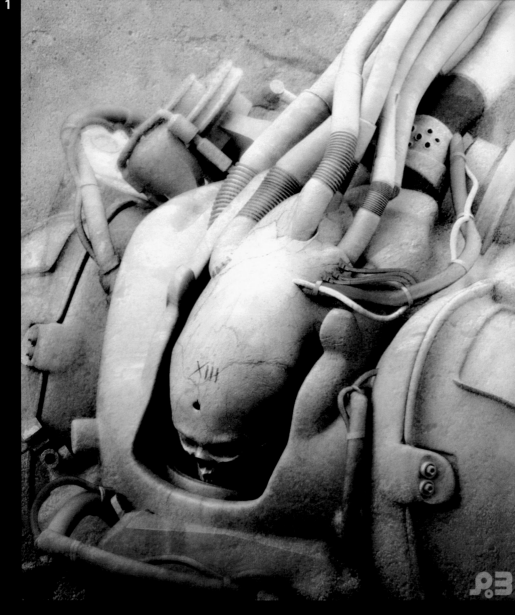

5

2

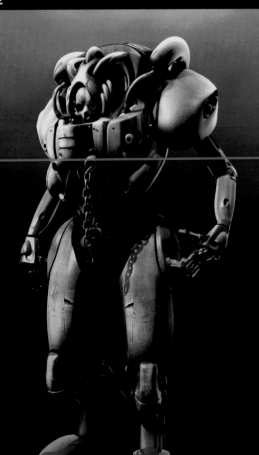

3

1
MoonJuju
LightWave, Photoshop
Joe Williamsen, Avalanche Software, USA

2
Stool
Maya
Steven Stahlberg, Malaysia

3
Bathing in the Night
3ds max, Deep Paint
Anatoliy Meymuhin, Russia

4
Phone Girl
Maya
Steven Stahlberg, Malaysia

1
Mantis
3ds max, Maya, Photoshop
Xiaobin Fang, China

2
Red eyed tree frog
3ds max, Photoshop
Mariska Vos, The Netherlands

3
Garden snail
CINEMA 4D, BodyPaint, Photoshop
Péter Fendrik, Hungary

4
Mantis
3ds max, Maya, Photoshop
Xiaobin Fang, China

1
Sunday Fluff XX
3ds max, VRay, Photoshop
Jimmy Maidens, USA

2
Two Penguins
Extreme 3D, trueSpace, Xara, Photoshop
Gary David Bouton, USA

3
RobotSalé
3ds max, finalRender, Photoshop
Caron Roland, France

4
Tusky the Unwakeable Walrus
Maya, Photoshop
Bryan Ballinger, USA

5
Love of Mermaid
Maya, Photoshop
Seong Gyu Jeon, GFX, Korea

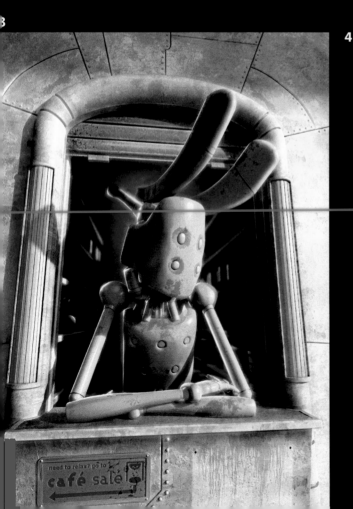

1
The Priest
Maya, Photoshop
David Smith, UK

2
Head
VIZ, finalRender, Photoshop
Marco Lazzarini, 3Dlink di Marco Lazzarini, Italy

3
Aristocrat
ZBrush
Marcel Laverdet, France

4
Pithecantrop
ZBrush
Marcel Laverdet, France

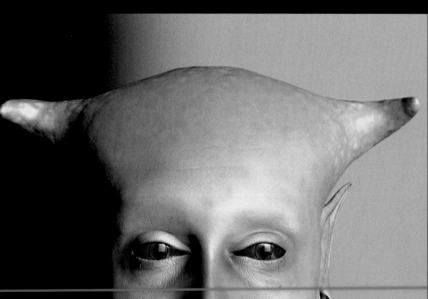

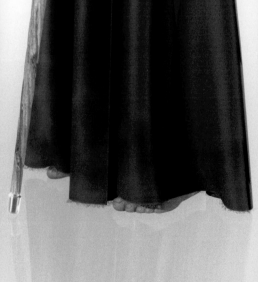

1

1
Old Lady
3ds max, Photoshop
Krishnamurti M. Costa, Brazil

2
Cane-Toad
Maya, Photoshop, inferno
David Clayton & Andrew Silke,
Cutting Edge VFX, Australia

3
Dragonstone
Maya, Photoshop
Leif Arne Petersen,
Loom Studios, Germany

4
The Freak
Maya, mental ray, Photoshop
Julian Johnson-Mortimer,
Picture-Art, UK

2

3

1

1
KiloByte
3ds max, Brazil, PhotoShop
Marcin Skrzypczak, Poland

2
Robo03
3ds max, XSI
Alessandro Briglia, Italy

3
Router
3ds max, Brazil, Photoshop
Ryan Lesser, USA

4
Mechanical Girl
Maya, Photoshop
Carlos Lin, Australia

5
Robo01
3ds max, XSI
Alessandro Briglia, Italy

2

4

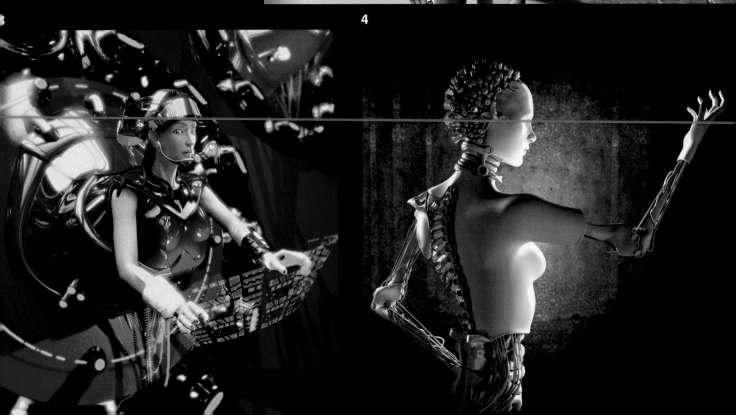

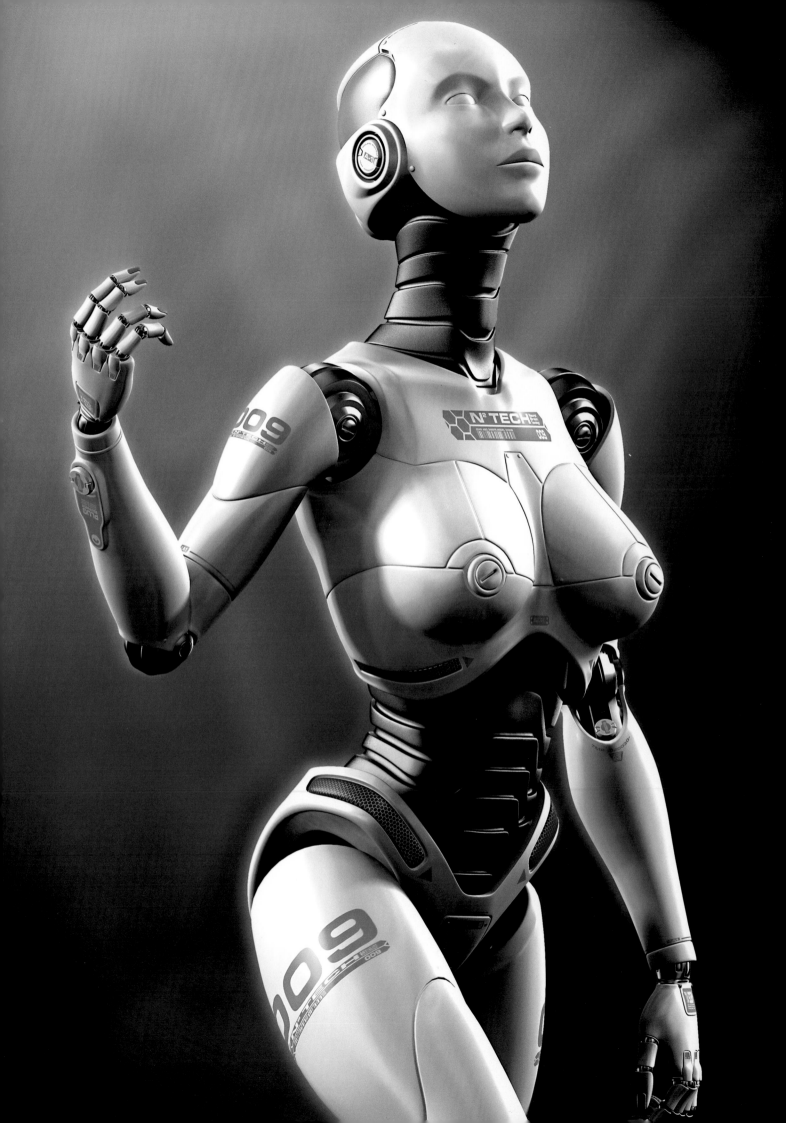

All that I loved is gone
Photoshop, Painter

The Blue Hour
Photoshop

1
Dogfight
Photoshop
Todd DeMelle, USA

2
Max
Photoshop
Tommie Löfqvist, Sweden

3
Baboon
Photoshop
Tommie Löfqvist, Sweden

4
Seraphim
Photoshop
Jason Alexander, USA

5
Last Descendant
Photoshop
Shawn Ye, Singapore

1
Fly Away
Photoshop, Painter
Agiostratitis Angelos, Greece

2
Whoose Got Yer Nose!!!
Photoshop
Robert Steinman, USA

3
Salvador Dali, autosodomised by His own Inspiration
Photoshop
Christos Neofotistos, Greece

4
The Crib
Client: Giant Studios
Photoshop, Maya, Shake
**Rodney Brunet, Candice Alger &
Douglas Lawrence**, TroubleMaker Studios, USA

César Romero '03

1
Straw, Sticks, Bricks
Photoshop
Ken Wong, Australia

2
Tax Collectors
Photoshop
Eric Wilkerson, USA

3
Ben the Bunny
Photoshop
Mikael Högström, Sweden

4
Oskar
Client: Lk Avalon
Painter
Maciej Wojtala, Poland

5
The Beast of Burden
Photoshop
Alain Paparone, France

yeah - boss
3ds max, Brazil
Vadim Pietrzynski, Spellcraft Studio, Germany

Praetorians Client: Pyro Studios
Brazil
Javier Abad, Jorge Blanco & Marcos Martinez, Semillitas, Spain

1
KONG
CINEMA 4D, Poser, Photoshop
Thierry Perrain, France

2
Elephants 2
Maya, mental ray, Shake
Balazs Kiss, UK

3
Ganesha
3ds max
Matt Clark, UK

4
Elephant
Maya, mental ray, Shake
Balazs Kiss, UK

5
carnivore
Photoshop, XSI
Daren Horley, Framestore-CFC, UK

2

4

3

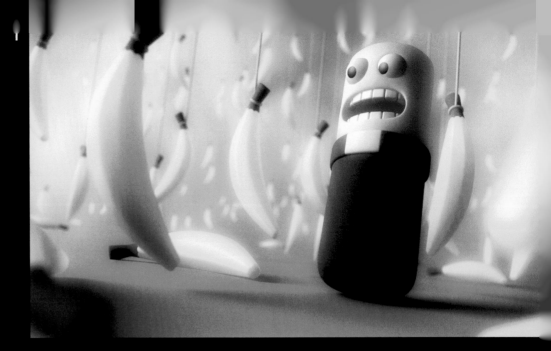

2

1
Fallen Angel
Client: Coprofago
3ds max, Photoshop
Neil Blevins, Soulburn Studios, USA

2
The Judge
LightWave, Photoshop
Gerard O'Dwyer, Ireland

3
Mother Nature (Winter)
Maya
Meats Meier, SketchOvision, USA

4
Mother Nature
Maya
Meats Meier, SketchOvision, USA

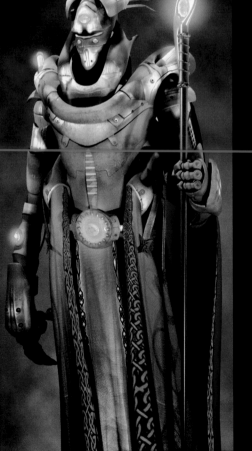

1

1
Travis in Action (Duality cover)
3ds max, Photoshop
**Alberto Gordillo &
Duality's graphic team**,
Trilobite Graphics, Spain

2
The Kiss
LightWave, Photoshop.
Robin Konieczny, Asylum 3D, UK

3
Fallen Angel
3ds max
Olivier Ponsonnet, France

4
Blue
Maya, Photoshop
**Christopher Mullins and Aaron
Webster**, USA

2

118 EXPOSÉ 1

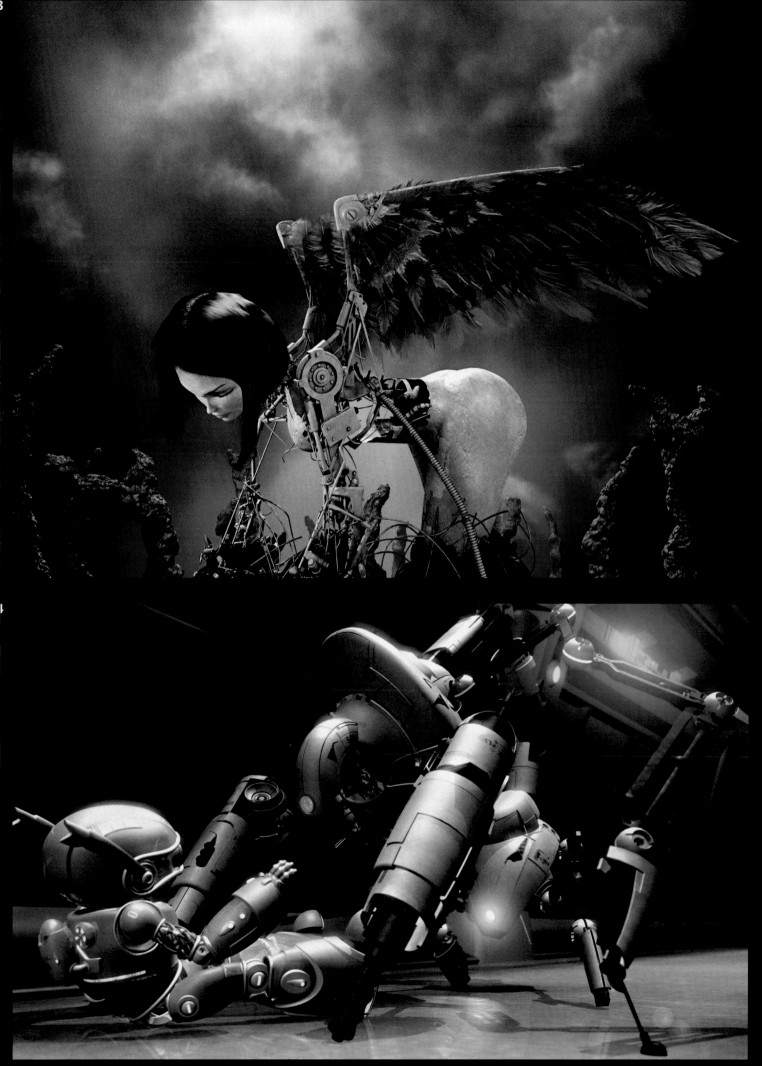

1
The wait is over...
3ds max, Photoshop
Jesus Pedrosa & Doug Chiang,
Next Limit, Spain

2
The White Rabbit
3ds max, Brazil, Photoshop
Tero Takalo & Jussi Saarela,
Outo Media, Finland

3
Pirate
3ds max, Photoshop
Matt Clark, UK

4
Circus Maximus Irritans
CINEMA 4D, BodyPaint, Photoshop
Péter Fendrik, Hungary

5
A Stop at the Estrian Plains
3ds max
Panya Souvanna, France

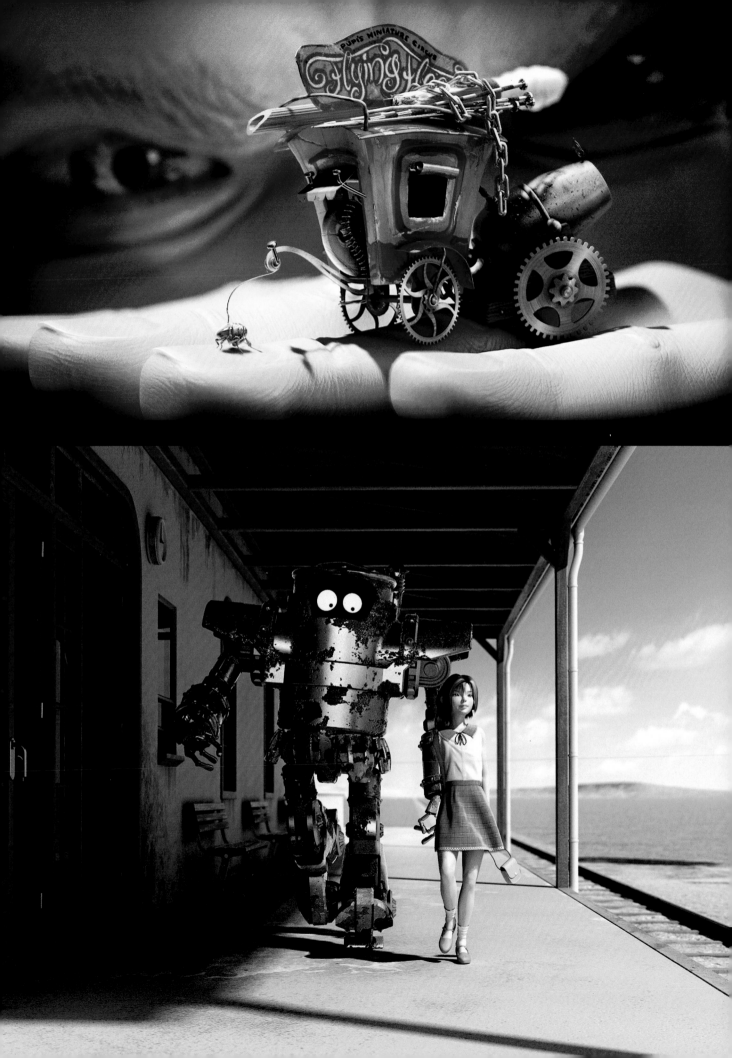

1

1
Underbrush
Photoshop
Christopher Cherubini, USA

2
Enchanted Forest
Client: Vivendi Universal Games
Photoshop, Painter
Philip Straub, USA

3
Gone Fishin
Client: Vivendi Universal
Photoshop, Painter
Philip Straub, USA

4
Tree of wisdom
Photoshop, Painter
Agiostratitis Angelos, Greece

5
Rainforest
Client: Vivendi Universal
Photoshop, Painter
Philip Straub, USA

2

3

2

3

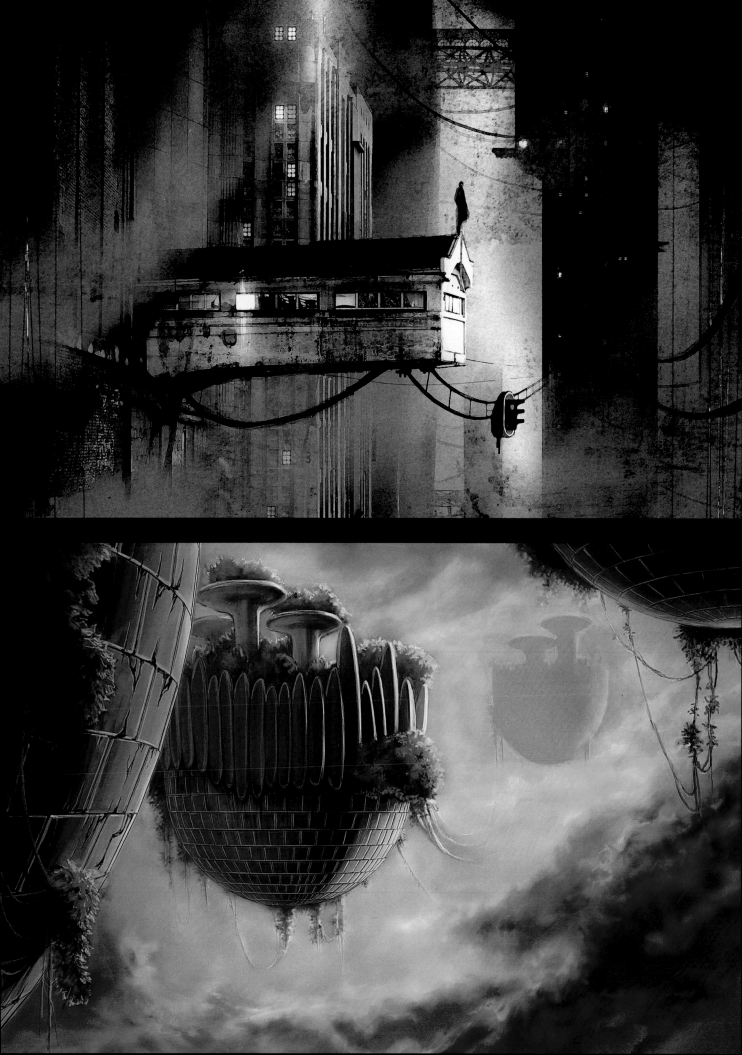

1
Somnio
Photoshop
Seung Ho Henrik Holmberg,
Sweden

2
Road Meeting
Painter
Caitlin Worth, USA

3
Forever Lost
Photoshop, Painter
Daniel Conway, UK

4
Levis Set Design
Photoshop
Seung Ho Henrik Holmberg,
The Moving Picture Company,
Sweden

1
Mountain Base
Photoshop
Seung Ho Henrik Holmberg,
Sweden

2
Dig
Photoshop
Seung Ho Henrik Holmberg,
Sweden

Leaving the Fifties
LightWave, Photoshop

Old England Morning
3ds max, Brazil, Photoshop, After Effects

2

1
Tunnel to Underworld
Client: Inflammatio Entretenimento
Photoshop
Mario Russo, Brazil

2
The Horde
Maya, mental ray, Photoshop
Balazs Kiss, UK

3
Island of the Romantic
XSI
Raphael Lacoste, Canada

4
Disorder
Terragen
Ensar Yanar, Turkey

1

1
Forest
3ds max, Photoshop
Olivier Archer, LBC, Honduras

2
A Malaysian Friday -
Kampung house exterior
LightWave, Photoshop
Tajino, Clickgrafix, Malaysia

3
Arctic Solstice
LightWave
Timothy Albee,
Timothy Albee Fine Art/Animation, USA

4
Enchanted Forest
3ds max, VRay, Photoshop
Andrzej Sykut, Poland

2

3

1
Depósito
3ds max, Photoshop
Juan Siquier, Spain

2
Gathering
3ds max
Alessandro Baldasseroni, Italy

3
Castle
Photoshop, Painter
Kim Hyun-Seung, Korea

4
Fluor
3ds max, Photoshop
Jocelyn Strob, Canada

1
My Rayz
Terragen
Ensar Yanar, Turkey

2
Militaristic Cityscape
Photoshop
Caitlin Worth, USA

3
Sea Shallows
Client: Academy of Arts
LightWave, Photoshop
Ray Sena, USA

4
Underwater
LightWave, Photo-Paint
Carlos Correia, Portugal

2

1

2

Canestra di Frutta
Universe

1

2

1

2

3

4

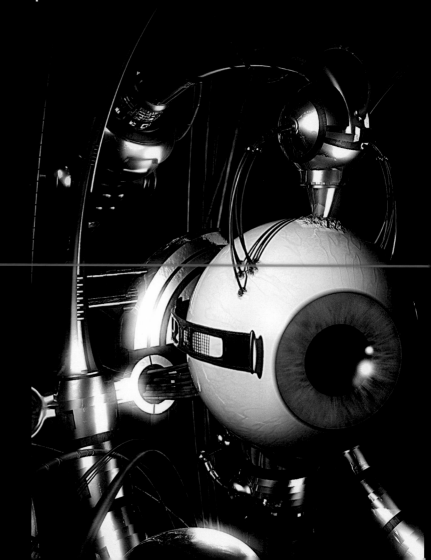

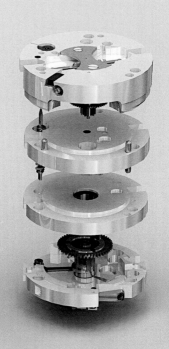
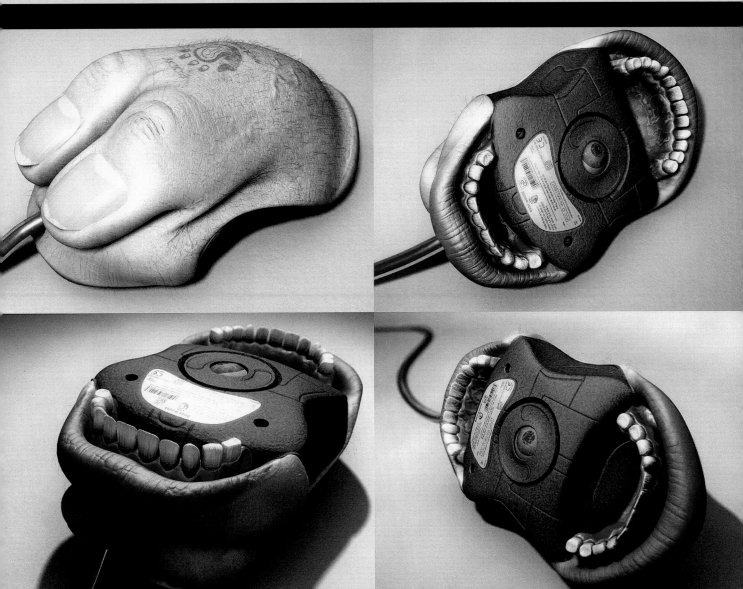

1

2

3

Uniracers
3ds max
Richard Green, Artbot, USA

People´s car
3ds max, Brazil, Photoshop

1
193X MG-P Series
LightWave, Photoshop
Nikos Gatos, Sweden

2
Porsche Boxter
3ds max, Photoshop
Aurel-Miron Manea, Romania

3
Power, Speed, and Beauty
3ds max, Brazil, Photoshop
Kevin Pazirandeh, USA

4
Bugatti EB110
Client: Shen Technologies
LightWave, Photoshop
Christelle Rouchaville, France

5
Audi RS6
3ds max, Photoshop
Simon Reeves, UK

6
Porsche GT3
LightWave, Photoshop
Leon Gaiazov, Canada

2

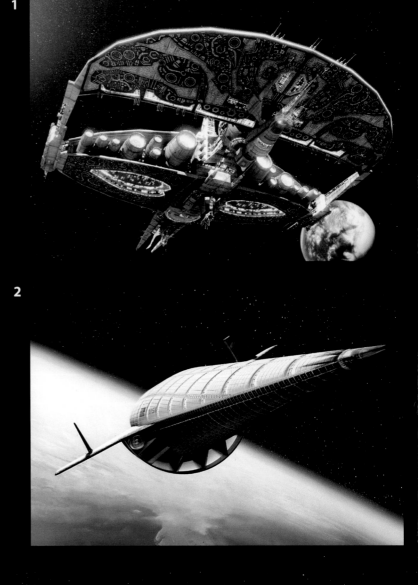

1
WAU2020 Spacecraft
LightWave, Photoshop
Tajino, Clickgrafix, Malaysia

2

Hyperion: Explore Magazine Cover
Client: University of Florida: Explore Magazine
LightWave, Photoshop
Nathan Phail-Liff, AlienintheBox, USA

3
Arrival
Photoshop
Gary Tonge, Vision Afar, UK

4
FIC Intel Packaging Art
Client: First International Computer of America
LightWave, Photoshop
Jo Watanabe & Nathan Phail-Liff,
AlienintheBox, USA

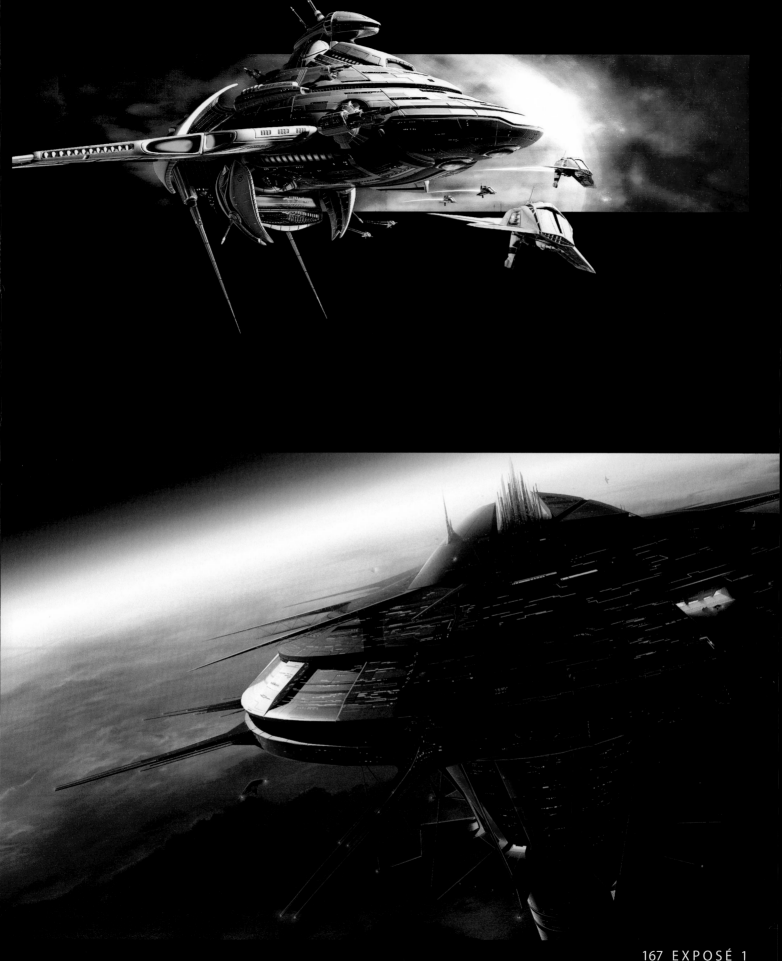

1

Honda S2000
Maya, 3ds max
Matthew Dartford, UK

2

Jaguar XJ220
LightWave
Jamie Clark, SamJam design,
USA

3

Audi TT Coupe Quattro
3ds max, finalRender, Photoshop
Stephen Jackson, UK

4

Porsche Boxter
3ds max, Photoshop
Aurel-Miron Manea, Romania

5

New Beetle
Rhino, 3ds max, VRay
Thomas Suurland, Denmark

1
Raybrig Honda NSX
3ds max
Morten Eric Munk Rowley,
Munkmotion, Australia

2
Ford Focus WRC
3ds max, Photoshop
Simon Reeves, UK

3
Peugeot 206 WRC 2000
Maya, 3ds max,
finalRender
Andrew Jackson, UK

4
Pennzoil Nismo
3ds max, VRay
Tom Winberg, WIDE,
Norway

5
*J.P. Montoya - Williams
BMW - FW 25*
Client: Allianz, Williams F1
LightWave
Christof Frank,
digi mice, Germany

1
Kingfisher
3ds max
Alessandro Baldasseroni, Italy

2
Snow Bike
Maya, Photoshop
Terry Stoeger, USA

3
Gripen
Photoshop
Seung Ho Henrik Holmberg, Sweden

4
One of the Last Swedish Steamtrains
CINEMA 4D, Vue d'Esprit, Photoshop
Stefan Harrysson, Sweden

5
The sleeping beast
3ds max, VRay, Photoshop
Dimitar Tzvetanov, Bulgaria

1
Caida libre
Photoshop
Alvaro Iglesias Sánchez, Spain

2
Above and Beyond
3ds max, VRay, Photoshop
Ila Soleimani, Iran

3
Lil' Chickwalker!
3ds max, Brazil
Jesse Sandifer, USA

4
turtle and mech
Photoshop
Aaron Krauss, USA

5
*Dashing Through The Snow
in a OneHorse OpenSleigh*
XSI, Renderman, Photoshop
Howard Gersh, USA

6
Kamikazi Cockroach
3ds max, Photoshop
Todd Dewsnup, USA

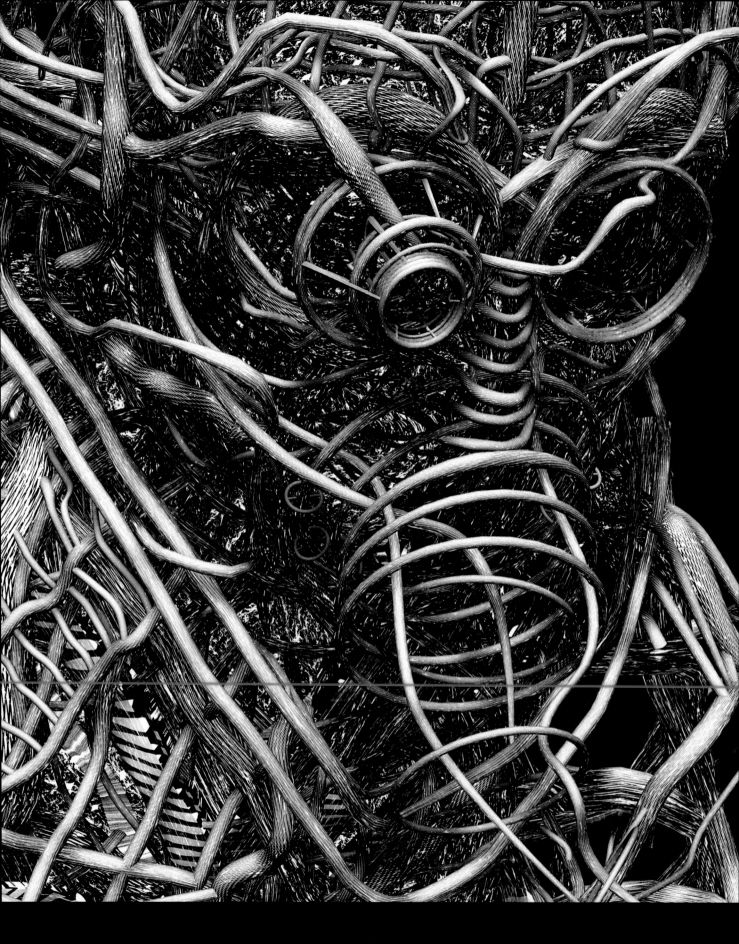

Etcher
Maya, Photoshop
Meats Meier, SketchOvision, USA

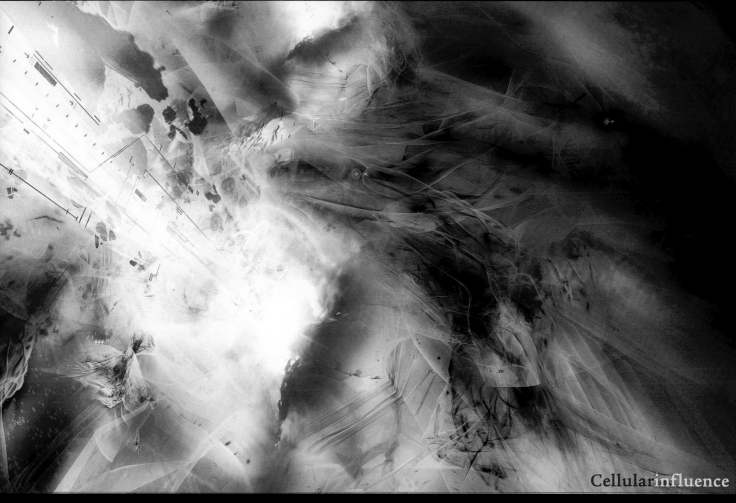

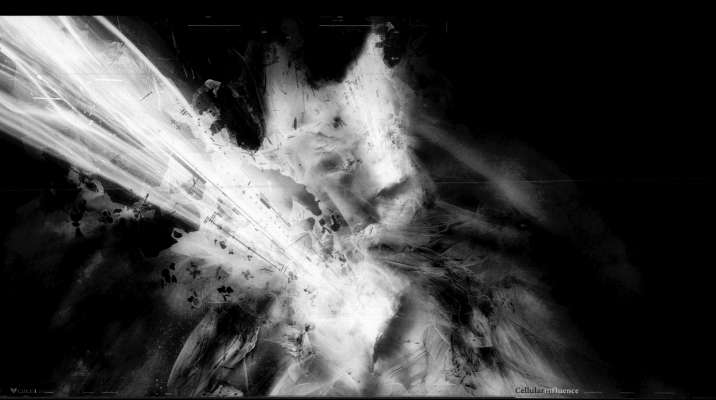

Cellular Influence
Client: Digital Vision, UK
3ds max, Photoshop, Illustrator
Jens Karlsson, Chapter Three, Sweden

1
Cloud Creation
LightWave, Photoshop
Ray Sena, LumenUmbra, USA

2
Microscope Shader
Realsoft 3D
Tim Borgmann,
BT-GRAFIK, Germany

3
Something in the Water
Painter
Mark Snoswell,
Snoswell Design, Australia

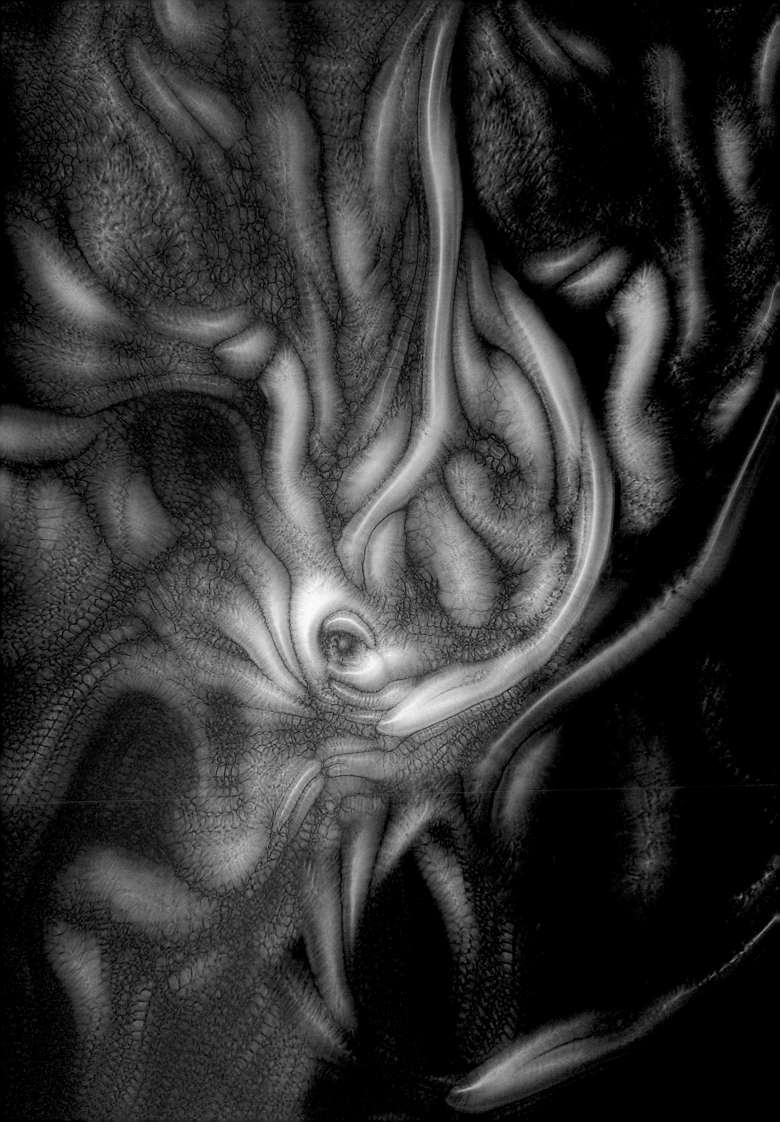

1
Pegasus II
3ds max, Photoshop, Illustrator
Jens Karlsson & James Widegren,
Chapter Three and Idiocase, Sweden

2
Spingatee
LightWave, Photoshop
Ray Sena, USA

3
LEVIATHAN
Client: Digital Vision, UK
3ds max, Illustrator, Photoshop
Jens Karlsson,
Chapter Three, Sweden

LEVIATHAN

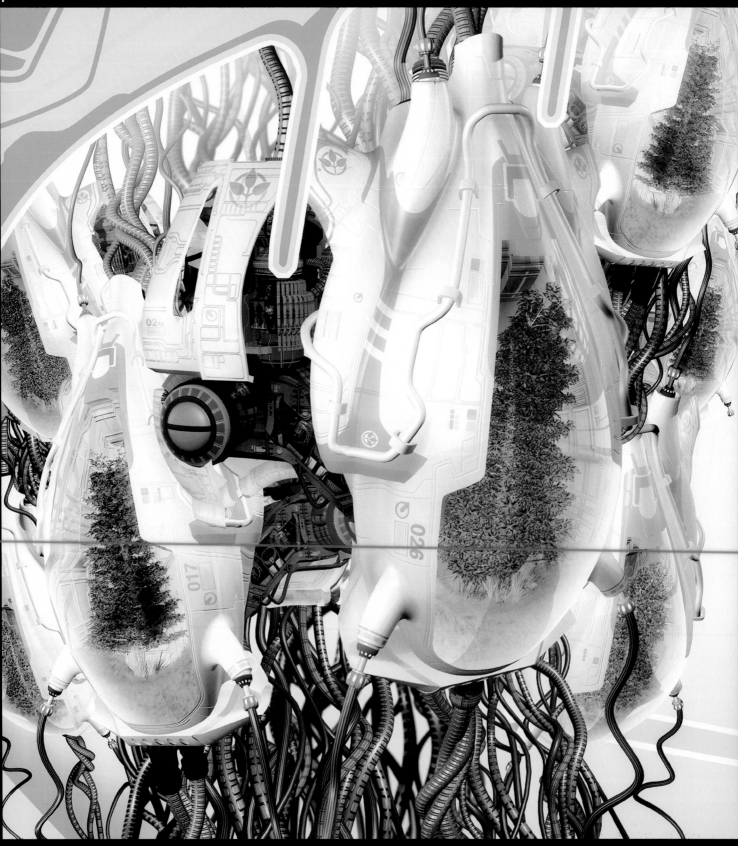

1
The Price of Magic
Photoshop
Steven Stahlberg, Malaysia

2
Ram Skulls
Maya, Photoshop
Meats Meier, SketchOvision, USA

3
Creation Digital Sculpture
Maya, Photoshop
Meats Meier, SketchOvision, USA

1
Etherlight
Photoshop
Gary Tonge, Vision Afar, UK

2
Self Residual
CINEMA 4D, 3ds max, Photoshop
Hugo O Delevante,
HOD Studio Films, USA

3 & 4
Fractal Flotsam
Painter
Mark Snoswell,
Snoswell Design, Australia

2

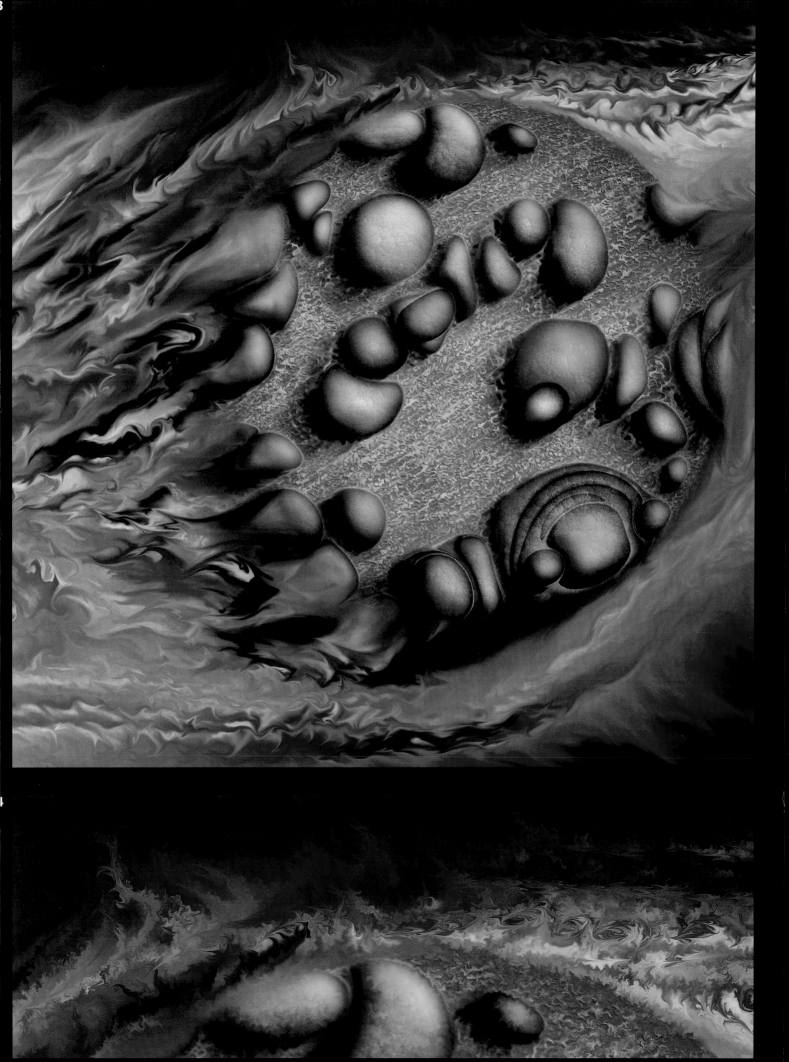

INDEX

Todd DeMelle
Boston MA
USA
ejwize@aol.com
96

Todd Dewsnup
527 South 100 East
Bountiful UT 84010
USA
www.roadsart.com
175

Rich Diamant
Amaze Entertainment
2801 Western Ave Apt 425
Seattle WA 98121
USA
www.rd3d.com
52

Juan Jose Gonzalez Diaz
Foncalada 10, 2ºA
Oviedo Asturias 33002
Spain
www.genesisvisual.com
20, 20, 36

Alan Dillingham
2614 M St.
Eureka CA 95501
USA
aln@mochamail.com
52

Katherine Dinger
2103 HWY 80 E #205
Mesquite TX 75150
USA
www.pocketmole.com
108

Kang Dong-Hyun
Wizard Soft
62-1 Chungdam-dong,
Kangnam-gu
Seoul 135-101
Korea
kasion@thrunet.com
73

Anders Ehrenborg
Gothenburg
Sweden
www.fellah.net
70

Xiaobin Fang
Beijing
China
fxb_jwy@etang.com
84, 85

Péter Fendrik
Angyal utca 4.
Budapest 1094
Hungary
fendrik@akcio.co.hu
63, 85, 121

Rudolf Fischer
Fischer Computeranimation
Bruchfeldstrasse 76
Frankfurt am main hessen
60528
Germany
www.specialvfx.com
151

Sawyer Fischer
Sawyer Fischer Rendering
1323 Henderson Way
Woodland CA 95776
USA
www.SFrendering.com
34

focus360
27123 Calle Arroyo
San Juan Capistrano CA 92675
USA
www.focus360.com
26, 153

Terry Ford
UK
www.terryf.dsl.pipex.com
66

Dean Fowler
4558 Willis Ave. #125
Sherman Oaks CA 91403
USA
www.machinephase.com
79

Christof Frank
digi mice
Hermannstrasse 34
Neu-Isenburg Hessen 63263
Germany
www.digimice.com
171

Anthony Fransella
463 Apple Tree Branch
Robbinsville North Carolina
28771
USA
www.antsin3d.com
54, 106

Maciej Frolow
Zaolzianska XI/6
Wroclaw Dolny Slask
Poland
www.nomad.4me.pl
151

Leon Gaiazov
410 boul St Joseph west
Montreal
Quebec H2V 2P2
Canada
gaiazov@hotmail.com
165

Markus Gann
Vordere Halde 40
Sindelfingen Baden
Württemberg 71063
Germany
www.begann.de
151

Nikos Gatos
Björnsonsgatan 52, IV
168 43 Bromma
Stockholm
Sweden
www.nikosgatos.com
164

Yohann da Geb
Avenida Doutor Timóteo
Penteado, 703Vila Progresso
Guarulhos SP
Brazil
www.yohann.com.br
146

Howard Gersh
Industrial Light + Magic
P.O. Box 2459
San Rafael CA 94912
USA
hgersh@ilm.com
175

Danny Geurtsen
139a Revelstoke Road
London Wimbledon Park
UK
danny@solarcoaster.eclipse
.co.uk
60

Marco Giubelli
MysticMan Productions
Via Pasquaro, 26
Varallo 13019
Italy
mysticman@libero.it
70, 70

Glintx
Glintxz2 CG studio
Room 701,No.14,1277 Lane,
Changning Road
Shanghai 200051
China
buby_wumy.nease.net
139, 156

Glintzz
Glintxz2 CG studio
Room 701,No.14,1277 Lane,
Changning Road
Shanghai 200051
China
buby_wumy.nease.net
156

Osvaldo Gonzalez
Pixelium
USA
www.pixelium-art.com
109, 126

Matthew Goodsell
341 Locust St.
Reno NV 89506
USA
www.goodsellart.com
50

Alberto Gordillo
Black & White studios
18 Chevremont, Jenner Road
Guildford Surrey
UK
gordillo.gfxartist.com
118

Richard Green
Artbot
7215 Plank Ave
El Cerrito CA 94530
USA
www.artbot.com
8, 162

Florian Guillaumot
17 Rue Emile Duployé
Bordeaux Gironde 33000
France
www.acidspeed.com
139

Micah Hancock
Syndrome Studio
Los Angeles CA
USA
www.syndromestudio.com
102, 182

Todd Harris
Avalanche Software
102 West 500 South, Suite 502
Salt Lake City UT 84109
USA
82

Stefan Harrysson
Hunnemarav. 18
37434 Karlshamn
Sweden
transfer.to/3d
172

Andrew Hartness
Ateliers Jean Nouvel
10, cité d'angoulême
Paris France 75011
France
www.jeannouvel.com
27, 27

James Hawkins
Legend Entertainment
Chantilly VA
USA
www.hawkprey.com
46

Jon Hey
Smoothe
Cairo Studios
4-6 Nile Street
London N1 7RF
UK
www.smoothe.com
24

Andy Hickes
Rendering.net
303 west 29th Street #B
New York NY 10001
USA
www.rendering.net
16, 39, 39, 39

Kit Hoang
Canada
kw@finestcard.com
107

Peter Hofmann
Heimgartenstraße 8
Weilheim 82362
Germany
www.3dluvr.com/pexel
159

Mikael Högström
Ersåsbacken 52
Gothenburgh - 42159
Sweden
www.duffe.nu/royal
105

Brent Holly
37849 Lakeshore Dr.
Harrison Twp MI 48045
USA
brenthollyusa@netscape.net
147

Seung Ho Henrik Holmberg
Sweden
henrik.cgcommunity.com
6, 128, 129, 131, 132, 132, 172

Daren Horley
Framestore-CFC
19-21 Wells Street
London
UK
www.framestore-cfc.com
113

Adam Howard
Invisiblecities
Ostlers Cottage, Stableblock,
Locksash Lane
West Marden West Sussex
UK
www.invisiblecities.co.uk
30

Vincent M. Hunter
WDG.Habib Architecture
750 North Saint PaulSuite 400
Dallas Texas 75201
USA
vhunter@weihe.com
18

Alexander Hupperich
LoomStudios
Kantstrasse 94
Berlin 10627
Germany
www.huppi.de
114

Kim Hyun-seung
103-1003 Dong-A apartment,
Kwan Ak Dream Town, Bong
Chun 5 Dong
Seoul Kwan Ak-Gu
Korea
www.khsbest.co.kr
47, 126, 145

Chris Jacks
Smoothe
2nd Floor, Bass Warehouse
Castle Street
Manchester M3 4LZ
UK
www.smoothe.com
21

Andrew Jackson
286 Scraptoft Lane
Leicester Leicestershire
UK
andyj.pdz@btopenworld.com
171

Stephen Jackson
286 Scraptoft Lane
Leicester
UK
Stevej@codemasters.com
168

Jaime Jasso
Metacube Studios
privada del niño 25b colonia
camino real
Zapopan Jalisco 45040
Mexico
www.metacube.com.mx
135, 135

Products credited by popular name in this book are listed alphabetically here by company.

Gerard O'Dwyer
'elm tree'
Tipperary Co.
Ireland
homepage.eircom.net/
~glsphere/
80, 116

Stephen Otvos
Otvos Illustration
Toronto Ontario
Canada
otvos_illustration@techie.com
44, 48, 108

Cemre Ozkurt
Blur Studios
711 Wilcox #201
Los Angeles CA 90038
USA
www.deluxepaint.net
57

P

Juan Jose Palomo
Paula De La Vega Nº18 Bajo E
Madrid 28036
Spain
www.3dblasphemy.com
74, 163

Alain Paparone
568, Boulevard Grignan
Toulon 83000
France
mapage.noos.fr/apaparone
105, 106

Jake Parker
2211 North Lamar Suite 100
Dallas TX 75202
USA
www.agent44.com
160

Fabrizio Pascucci
Simbiosi
via xxv aprile 42/a
Fiesole Fi 50014
Italy
www.simbiosi.com
28

Kevin Pazirandeh
566 Muskingum Ave
Pacific Palisades CA 90272
USA
kevin@kzone3d.com
164

Jesus Pedrosa
Next Limit
Claudio Coello 81, 3º A exterior
Madrid 28001
Spain
www.geocities.com/SoHo/
Gallery/1015/
120

Chris Pember
Winnpeg, Manitoba
Canada
www.3dluvr.com/gunnah
136

Don Perkins
don perkins illustration
437 Morning Glory Court
Wilmington NC 28405
USA
www.donperkins.com
61

Thierry Perrain
France
perso.wanadoo.fr/
perrain3dportfolio/
112, 137

Leif Arne Petersen
Loom Studios
Lietzensee Ufer 6
Berlin 14057
Germany
www.cgeye.de
90

Nathan Phail-Liff
AlienintheBox
USA
www.alieninthebox.com
166, 167

Paul Pham
80 Kane St. Apt. A3
West Hartford CT 06119
USA
www.paul-pham.com
124, 125

Vadim Pietrzynski
Spellcraft Studio
Senefelder Str. 23
Berlin 10437
Germany
www.yeahthemovie.de
110

Olivier Ponsonnet
53 rue Hoche 33200 Bordeaux
Bordeaux 33200
France
reiv.fr.st
119, 137

John Pruden
Digital-X
10201 S. 51st Street Suite 245
Phoenix AZ 85044
USA
www.digitalx3d.com
5, 22, 28, 34, 153

Q

Chen Qingfeng
Room 201,
No.990-1,Xiahe Road,
Xiamen Fujian 361004
China
www.highend3d.com/artists/
artist.3d?au=chenqingfeng&
iid=159
19, 24, 33, 38, 146

R

Benoit de Ravel "Bengal"
19 Rue des Bons Raisins
92500 Rueil Malmaison
France
www.cafesale.net/bengal
41

Simon Reeves
15 Savernake Avenue
Melksham Wiltshire
UK
www.simonreeves.co.uk
165, 170

Dalius Regelskis
UAB Design Solutions
Kalvariju St 1
Vilnius
Lithuania
www.cad-services.biz
32

Lars Ribbum
NBBJ-HUS-PKA Architects
22

Caron Roland
25 rue de macon
Alfortville France 94140
France
r.caron.free.fr
86

Cesar Romero
Carlos Lopez #370Col. Lomas
de Santa Maria
Morelia Michoacan 58090
Mexico
www.3dluvr.com/cero
103

Jiaxing Rong
1713 Benson Ave
Brooklyn NY 11214
USA
www.jrtistic.com
44

Mario Rothenbühler
i Design
Poststrasse 10
Biberist Solothurn 4562
Switzerland
www.i-design.ch
7

Christelle Rouchaville
254 Bld Voltaire
Paris 75011
France
christeller@noos.fr
76, 165

Morten Eric Munk Rowley
Munkmotion
10/70-72 Jenner St
Baulkham Hills NSW 2153
Australia
www.munkmotion.com
170

Mario Russo
R: Gago Coutinho, 1087
Londrina Paraná
Brazil
mrussoart@yahoo.com
140

S->

Jussi Saarela
Outo Media
Kajaaninkatu 25 A 8
Oulu - 90100
Finland
saarela@archeus.fi
120

Sami Salo
Itäinen rantakatu 60 a A 17
20810 Turku
Finland
sami.salo@auriamail.net
75

Alvaro Iglesias Sánchez
Travesía del Grillo, Nº 2, 5ºA
Torrelavega (Cantabria) 39300
Spain
artealvaro.tripod.com
130, 174

Jesse Sandifer
Dallas TX
USA
jessesandifer@juno.com
174

Mars Sandoval
Syndrome Studio
Los Angeles CA
USA
www.syndromestudio.com
102, 183, 183

Bang SangHyun
OMIX studio
HwangHwa B/D 1301,
Yoeksam-dong 832-7,
KangNam-ku,Seoul
South Korea
www.omixstudio.com
66, 66

Victor Ruiz Santacruz
www.twistedesign.com
7, 160

Markus Schille
Aasvegen 4
Moss Ostfold
Norway
home.no/markuss
79

Sedone
USA
www.sedone.com
56

Ray Sena
3704 Anza Way
San Leandro CA 94578
USA
raysena.clan-510.org
130, 149, 178, 180

Steven Shmuely
15 Strathton Manor,
Helen Close, Strathavon
Johannesburg Gauteng 2031
South Africa
lucid@icon.co.za
58

Andrew Silke
Cutting Edge VFX
56 Morley St
Toowong QLD 4066
Australia
www.cane-toad.com
90

Juan Siquier
C/Muelle 9, 4ºIzq.
Albacete 2001
Spain
www.juansiquier.com
144

Marcin Skrzypczak
Kosnego13/8
Opole
Poland
viollus@poczta.fm
5, 92

David Smith
20 Grenaby Avenue,
Croydon, Surrey
UK
dave@thepolysmith.com
88

Mark Snoswell
Snoswell Design
Australia
www.cgCharacter.com
179, 187, 187

Maria Sokolova
Klovsky Spysk street,#12,flat
#5
Kiev 1021
Ukraine
kisa2705@yahoo.com
54

Ila Soleimani
apt.13, Saba building, 15th st.,
Velenjak
Tehran
Iran
www.ilasolomon.com
68, 174

Panya Souvanna
Orléans 45000
France
spady@free.fr
121

Steven Stahlberg
7-6-2 Menara Hartamas
Sri Hartamas
50480 Kuala Lumpur
Malaysia
www.optidigit.com/stevens
1, 55, 82, 83, 95, 184

Robert Steinman
227 Rachel Court
Franklin Park NJ 08823
USA
www.taminglight.com
100, 108, 130

Pierre St-Hilaire
My Virtual Model
6745 de Lorimier
Montréal Québec
Canada
sthash@sympatico.ca
42

Terry Stoeger
620 Niagara Lane N
Plymouth MN 55447
USA
home.attbi.com/~tstoeger/
139, 150, 158, 158

Philip Straub
1355 Blvd. Apt. 4
West Hartford CT 06119
USA
www.philipstraub.com
50, 124, 124, 125

Jocelyn Strob
255 rue Prince-Edouard
Quebec Qc
Canada
www.strob.net
145

Thomas Suurland
Denmark
www.suurland.com
169

Andrzej Sykut
Poland
www.azazel.f2o.org
56, 143